# Catfishing Secrets

*Your Practical Catfishing Tips Guide To
Catching The Big Catfish*

# Bowe Packer

# TABLE OF CONTENTS

# PUBLISHERS NOTES

### Disclaimer

This publication is intended to provide helpful and informative material on catfishing. It is not intended to cover every aspect of this sport.

Please understand the author made every attempt to provide sound and practical information that will assist you with catching big catfish. You will undoubtedly run into things the author did not. That is the natural process of life.

No action should be taken solely on the contents of this book. Always consult your physician or qualified health-care professional on any matters regarding your health and before adopting any suggestions in this book or drawing inferences from it.

The author and publisher specifically disclaim all responsibility for any liability, loss or risk, personal or otherwise, which is incurred as a consequence, directly or indirectly, from the use or application of any contents of this book.

Any and all product names referenced within this book are the trademarks of their respective owners. None of these owners have sponsored, authorized, endorsed, or approved this book.

Always read all information provided by the manufacturers' product labels before using their products. The author and publisher are not responsible for claims made by manufacturers.

**Kindle Edition 2013**

Manufactured in the United States of America

# DEDICATION

I dedicate this book to all those people out there who remind us of the things we have forgotten about ourselves.

And this holds especially true of my beautiful and amazing wife, Alma. She is the one woman who has the most amazing talent to let me grow and love the things about myself that I have not fully accepted.

I cherish the love she has for me when I may not know how to love myself.

May we all have this kind of beautiful soul in our life.

Sent from LOVE,

Sunshine In My Soul

# HOW TO GET THE MOST OUT OF THIS BOOK

So you're looking to find out more information about catfishing. Fishing of all types is fun for people of all ages but this book is going to focus strictly on the catfishing and how it can be done whether you're a beginner or an expert.

Are you looking to become an expert angler? Well then this book will help you to do exactly that. You're going to learn the tips and tricks that expert anglers have been using for decades. You'll also find out everything you need to know about lakes, rivers and all the different types of catfish you'll find in the different parts of the world.

In Part 1 of this book you'll find out all you need to know about catfish. That means you'll learn what a catfish is, how they live and what they do to survive. You'll even find out about the many different types of catfish that live in Asia, North America and even South America. In fact there are far too many types of catfish for us to even mention in this short book. So we'll focus on a few of the most well-known and widespread.

The largest catfish in the United States have their own section here. Find out everything from eating habits to breeding habits and even how to determine the age of your catfish. All of these things are discussed throughout Part 1 of this book.

In Part 2 we'll talk about the way that you're going to go out and start fishing for yourself. This is where we're going to get into all the tips that you need to become one of the best anglers. You'll also learn about what catfishing really is and how you can enjoy it. Start having fun and adventure whether you're going out by yourself or going out with the group. So have some fun and get learning.

# PART 1: INTRODUCTION – THE CATFISH

Catching that elusive catfish is no easy task as any experienced angler will tell you. But it is something that is well worth your time and effort. You'll have fun and you'll definitely be relaxing by the water for a good, long time.

So why would you want to spend all those hours and all that time and effort trying to catch a catfish? Because of the joy and the love of the sport. So many anglers put hours into their fishing trips and lots of money into their lines, poles and other equipment in hopes of catching this amazing, hard to trap, fish. It's about the dedication and the excitement when you finally catch one and can show it off to everyone you know.

The thrill and the excitement are what draw so many new people to this sport and they are what keeps the old-hats continuing on day after day and week after week. You'll feel that same excitement the tenth time that you feel the first or the second because not everyone can succeed at this sport and you can.

## WHY IS CATFISHING SO GREAT?

So why is catfishing better than any other type of fishing? Well a large number of anglers around the world will give you some great reasons. Topping the list is the simple sport of it all. After all, catfish are not the easiest fish to catch and you'll need skill in order to snag one. That's the goal of any fisherman after all, showing off their skills.

So you may be wondering, 'why catfish? Why not some other fish? After all there are hundreds of different kinds right?' You would be right of course. There are far more species of fish than we could ever imagine. But catfish are very special to the anglers who fish for them for a few different reasons.

A catfish is very hardy and it's highly adaptable. It's adapted for decades to live in rivers and ponds around the world and it's adapted to far more than that. These are powerful fish that grow at tremendous rates. In fact they could put on more than three pounds each year. Of course the bigger the fish the harder it is to catch since they put up even more of a fight. You'll have to have skill to pull in one of these but you'll definitely be glad of it because that fish will taste great when you get it cooked and on your plate.

So where can you find one of these catfish? Like we said, they're found all over the world in all types of water and all types of conditions. But just because they're common doesn't mean you can easily reel one in. Getting it on the line may be simple but keeping it there long enough to get it in the boat will be another story entirely. These fish can rip out lines, tear up bait and more breaking away from capture.

## MEET YOUR TARGET

So what do you need to know in order to catch that elusive catfish? Well one of the biggest things you need to know is the catfish itself. You can't expect to just put your line in one day and hook one. You need to know everything you possibly can bout this fish. That's what any true catfish angler will tell you after all. So let's get into learning about the catfish, what it is and what it does.

The morphology of the catfish (that's a fancy way of saying the way that it looks) is quite unique. The ones that live in the United States at least have barbells or what seem to be whiskers sticking out of the sides of its face. This is where the original name came from of course and it stuck. These whiskers however, much like the whiskers of your cat, are actually very important to the fish itself.

The whiskers (known in more professional circles as barbells) allow the fish to feel and taste what is around it. This shows them where food is and more importantly where danger is. No matter where they are or what type of environment they are exposed to, these fish are capable of using their barbells to sense what's near them.

So what else should you know about the barbells on these catfish? Well for one thing, they can't hurt you. Many people falsely believe that the barbells of a catfish can cause pain and are used to attack. The barbells are used for finding food and danger however they are not used to fight. These fish instead have barbs in their dorsal and pectoral regions which allow them to fight off enemies. You won't be hurt by the barbells but you could still be hurt by this fish. That's because the barbs can puncture the skin and cause a great deal of pain.

There are even many of these species of fish that have cells full of venom to help them fend off predators of all different types. Because of these defence mechanisms this fish is able to live a long life and it's capable of surviving in the most dangerous parts of the world and the water.

Unlike many species of fish, catfish don't have scales covering their body. Instead, they simply have skin (like humans) though theirs is rough and made up of armoured plates. These are much tougher than the scales that other fish possess and are required because of the depths and murky waters where these fish live. Of all the two thousand species of catfish (and there are thousands of each of those catfish) none of them have scales at all. The plates however (that not all catfish have) are stronger than regular scales could ever be.

## SEEING THE WORLD FROM THE EYES OF A CATFISH

So if catfish don't have scales and don't look as good as some of the other fish how do they get around? How do they survive and experience the different aspects of the world as we know it? Well these fish have amazing skill in several areas that allow them to actually prosper even better than the other fish that we've seen in the past.

- Superior sense of taste
- Superior sense of smell
- Superior sense of sight
- Superior sense of hearing

Yes those are all traits that a catfish has over a regular fish. They are capable of seeing, hearing and tasting in the deep murky waters that they call home (though their sight is severely limited by those murky waters). This is why the sense of taste, hearing and smell come in handy in these areas. These senses make up for the fact that visibility in the deep, dark water is only a few inches.

Now here's how everything works together so that this fish can make its way through the water and also make its way to finding food and avoiding danger. If you've ever watched a body of water you know that it continually moves. There are always ripples of some type even if they aren't full-blown waves. Well those ripples are happening below the surface as well. The catfish can tell what's happening because it uses its nose to accept incoming and outgoing water.

Inside the nose are tissues that are capable of, as your nose is, smelling the water. It can smell whether there is prey nearby or if there is some type of danger nearby. If either of these things occur the fish is able to react properly. Of course not all catfish have the abilities that others do. Some of them may have less ability in terms of smelling though all of them have excellent abilities in other regards.

This fish is capable of smelling nearly anything. In fact, its senses are so good it can pick up a scent that is 1/1,000,000,000 parts of water. It can single out what every individual smell is down to that tiny degree so that it knows what it's after is food or whether it's a predator.

But that's not all that this incredible fish has to protect itself and seek out food. It also has an extremely advanced sense of taste as well. This is because the catfish has taste buds throughout its entire body. These taste buds appear throughout the gills, mouth, belly, dorsal region and fins as well. That's so that the catfish can taste the water and pinpoint where anything is. Remember that amazing sense of smell? Well this sense of taste is amazing as well. And it explains why catfish can grow to six hundred pounds.

So what else is there? A fish with such amazing senses of smell and taste couldn't possibly need anything else could it? Well as a matter of fact it may not *need* anything else, but it certainly has it. This fish is capable of hearing very well under the water. It doesn't have ears in the traditional sense that you would think of and they certainly don't look like human ears. Instead, this fish has sound receptors.

It also has amazing sound receptors that are far stronger than anything that any other fish has. Think about it this way. An average trout has sound receptors capable of picking up auditory vibrations of up to one thousand cycles per second. That sounds like quite a bit doesn't it? And it's probably decent for underwater hearing right? Well a catfish has the ability to hear thirteen thousand cycles per second. That's because it has not only a set of regular sound receptors but also a lateral line of backup hearing that can hear even more than the regular receptors can. This line goes from the top of the head down to the jaw and it's very important. Why is that? Well because it helps the catfish sense:

1. Members of the same species of catfish
2. Larger fish
3. Prey
4. Danger above the water

All of these things will help the fish to find food and avoid danger as well as locate potential 'friends.' This sensitivity to vibrations has been shown through use of catfish to predict earthquakes and even captive ones to detect when someone is approaching the pond. That's because these catfish can feel the vibrations in the ground and even beneath the ground.

So we're on to the last of the senses. The sense of sight. Now these fish live in deep, murky water and when you look at them they may seem to have poor eyesight because of the look of their eyes. If you think this however, you definitely can't be more mistaken. These catfish actually see very well whether they are in light or dark water. They can even sense the electromagnetic field of the creatures around them even if they can't actually see them. This definitely makes them different from other species of fish and other animals entirely.

## CATFISH ALL AROUND THE WORLD

So how many types of catfish are there around the world? Well as we've already told you there are quite a lot. But of course it would take hundreds of pages to talk about all of them. Instead, we're going to focus on a few of the more common or more popular ones so that we can get some good information to you without boring you with pages on fish you may never see.

| Name | Special Characteristics |
|------|------------------------|
| Mekong Catfish | This fish grows up to twelve feet though it grows to be heavier than other types of catfish. In fact it's been recorded at up to 650 pounds.<br><br>Most of these fish are found in Southeast Asia though they are only near certain areas of this country. A freshwater fish, these are definitely a force to be |

| | |
|---|---|
| | reckoned with. |
| Sheatfish | This is one of the bigger catfish that you will find. In fact, it can grow up to 15 feet long and weigh up to six hundred pounds. That's definitely a big fish and it's found in nearly all flowing, freshwater bodies of water in the European countries.<br><br>This fish eats a wide range of other fish and even small mammals. In fact, it's been known to snatch up birds and even dogs from the water. So be careful of your pets while you hunt this fish. |
| South American Catfish | As the name suggests this catfish is found in areas of South America. It's actually not one specific type at all but a few different species. Some of these, like the azulejo species grow up to 200 pounds. |

| Goonah Catfish | India is the South Asian country most known for this catfish. It's been shown in movies and documentaries for many years and grows to be the size of a full grown human, approximately 5 feet long and 150 pounds.<br><br>Known as a stalker this fish has been blamed for capturing and devouring children though these claims are entirely false. It does however have large and powerful jaws. |
| Upside Down Catfish | This fish is known for exactly the reason you would think based on the name. It's actually capable of swimming completely upside down. Not only is it able to but it actually does swim upside down once it becomes an adult. At this point in time the lower |

| | |
|---|---|
| | section of the fish (the top) becomes darker in colour. This fish is found mainly in Africa. |
| Electric Catfish | Found mainly in Africa this fish is smaller than most of the others. In fact it only grows to about fifty pounds. Of course it does have another way to protect itself because the electric catfish can send up to 300 volts of electricity through its body. |
| Talking Catfish | This fish is called a talking catfish because it's able to emit a sound by rubbing two of the bones in its body together producing a high-pitched call. This fish is generally found in freshwater located in South America. |
| Candiru | This fish is generally found in the Amazon River or other freshwater throughout South America. It's a small fish comparative to other catfish however it's |

|  | a very dangerous one. |
| --- | --- |
|  | The Candiru is known as a parasite because it will smell for a specific chemical trace and then attach itself to the gills of the fish that produces that chemical. This fish stick out spikes once it gets inside the gills and sucks the blood of the fish it's attached to. |
| Glass Catfish | Found in Asia these fish are actually able to be kept as pets because they are smaller than most others. They are also very interesting fish because they are completely transparent until their death. They are capable of living in any freshwater. |
| The Big Three | This is, again, not just one fish but a group of them. In fact there are three common United States fish found in this category. They are the blue catfish, channel catfish and flathead catfish. |

| | They are also large fish that are sometimes too heavy to be caught. |
|---|---|

## TOP OF THE CATFISH FOOD CHAIN

Within the United States there are 45 different species of catfish. That may sound like a lot but remember how many different species we said there were earlier? Well 45 is a pretty small fraction of that. This is why having "The Big Three" is so great for the U.S. The three biggest catfish that we have however, are definitely very large.

These fish are some of the largest in the world and they are definitely ones that will give you a challenge and a run for your money. Beginners and experienced anglers alike love to go for these giant fish. Because they're so common in this area and they are some of the more popular, large fish to catch, this section will focus on these three fish.

# CHAPTER 1- THE CHANNEL CATFISH – THE FIRST BIG GIANT

The official Latin name of this huge fish is *Ictalarus Punctatus* though it's more commonly referred to as the channel catfish. It's the most popular of all the types of catfish within the United States though it has been known by several different names.

- Fiddler Catfish
- Speckled Catfish
- Eel Catfish
- Willow Catfish
- Great Lake Catfish
- And many more!

## IDENTIFICATION

So how do you know if you've found a channel catfish rather than some other type? Well there are a few ways that you can distinguish this fish from any other species. Catfish are all going to look similar to one another though you should know that there will be slight differences based on the type of water they live in and the type of environment as well. However those slight differences allow you to identify this fish if you look closely enough.

For one thing this is considered a nicer looking version at least of the big three. It's a little more sleek and it's definitely a prettier colour than the others. There are a variety of different colours available however with some appearing in a silver while others are dark brown. All of them have a white belly which contrasts with whichever colour they happen to be.

But there is more to know about the colour of these fish. In fact, the colour will typically change as the fish gets older. The younger fish may have silvery skin and speckles but this will start to change as it gets older. The speckles fade away and males will turn a dark blue. There are other differences in males as they get older as well. They will develop a larger head and thicker lips indicating that they are of a breeding age.

Allowing catfish to breed in your area is important so you want to avoid catching (or at least keeping) males who are of this breeding age. They are not the same as blue catfish though they will look similar this point in their life. The difference between these two is in the anal fin. The channel catfish have 24-29 rounded spikes on this fin while the blue catfish has over 30 straight spines.

Other ways to identify this fish are by the speckles on the head or by their forked tails. Other types of catfish do not have this forked tail and also don't have the developed upper jaw which extends over the lower jaw. These are some of the best ways to ensure that it is, in fact, a channel fish that you've caught.

If you're looking for these types of catfish you can look just about anywhere in the United States. They've been seen nearly everywhere but Alaska. However they are also found in other freshwater bodies of water including Mexico and large portions of Canada.

## HOW IT GROWS

So you're probably wondering a little more about this particular type of fish. Well there are a lot of different things to know. For one thing, the channel catfish grows to only about one to five pounds. In some areas it grows closer to six-ten pounds but only in Arkansas and Mississippi has it been found over 40 pounds. These catfish are definitely the largest you will find anywhere and have won trophy's for the anglers who find them. In other areas of the country you would be lucky to find one as large as 20 pounds.

The maximum lifespan of a channel catfish is approximately 20 years though most do not live past the ten year mark. Those kept in captivity rarely last past this age. There is definitely an interaction between the weight and length of these fish as well as their age and the growth rate is found to be slower than with other types of catfish. The tables below will tell you about these associations though it's important to keep in mind these are only the average correlations.

| Length of Catfish | Average Weight |
| --- | --- |
| 12 inches | .5 pound |
| 15 inches | 1.3 pounds |
| 18 inches | 2.7 pounds |
| 21 inches | 3.3 pounds |
| 24 inches | 5.8 pounds |
| 27 inches | 8.8 pounds |
| 33 inches | 15.3 pounds |
| 36 inches | 20.4 pounds |

| Age of Catfish (Northern US Catfish) | Length of Catfish |
|---|---|
| 1 year old | 5.7 inches |
| 2 years old | 7.1 inches |
| 3 years old | 9 inches |
| 4 years old | 10.5 inches |
| 5 years old | 12.3 inches |
| 6 years old | 14.1 inches |
| 7 years old | 15.9 inches |
| 8 years old | 18.4 inches |
| 9 years old | 19.7 inches |

| Age of Catfish (Southern US Catfishes) | Length of Catfish |
|---|---|
| 1 year old | 10.9 inches |
| 2 years old | 13.7 inches |
| 3 years old | 15.7 inches |
| 4 years old | 17.8 inches |
| 5 years old | 19 inches |
| 6 years old | 21.6 inches |
| 7 year old | 22.6 inches |
| 8 years old | 23.5 inches |

| 9 years old | 24.3 inches |

This shows that there is definitely a size difference between Northern and Southern ranges for these fish as well as showing the rates by year.

## HABITATS OF THE CHANNEL CATFISH

The next thing you're probably wondering is where to find these giant fish. Well the best places are freshwater ponds, lakes of all sizes, freshwater impoundments, artificial ponds, unpolluted creeks and rivers in lowland regions. These fish *will* live in dirty and polluted water however they thrive best in clean and clear water. The best chance to catch one is in that clear water.

If you're looking to find these catfish you can seek out murky waters because chances are that within the United States you may find them there. You won't find any that will win you trophies however as the fish living in these polluted conditions typically don't grow very large. The bigger fish are in cleaner and clearer bodies of water with moderate currents. Those currents allow the catfish to hide. Another point to look out for is the water temperature.

Channel catfish prefer water that is between 75 and 80 degrees Fahrenheit so check the water temperature before you start spending too much time. Lower water makes these catfish become more and more lazy until they simply sink to the bottom of the water. You'll never catch them that way. Under 50 degrees Fahrenheit you aren't likely to catch a channel catfish because they simply aren't eating.

## FEEDING THE CHANNEL CATFISH

After dark is the prime feeding time of these fish and it's also when these fish start getting more active and swimming toward more shallow water. During the day when it's bright and hottest out these fish are more sedentary, relaxing in rocks and other hiding places. These places allow them to relax and stay cool and safe. Of course the important thing then is to know what these fish eat.

> ➢ Aquatic and terrestrial insects
> ➢ Mussels
> ➢ Live salamanders
> ➢ Small frogs
> ➢ Moth and butterfly caterpillars
> ➢ Small to mid-sized fish
> ➢ Freshwater leeches
> ➢ Earthworms
> ➢ Crayfish

As you may have guessed from the list here there are quite a large range of foods that you can use for bait. These fish will even eat organic matter or even dead fish if they can't find their primary food sources. It takes very little for them to survive and continue to grow. No matter how little food they are capable of getting for themselves these fish will easily grow to the averages we discussed above. In fact it doesn't even matter if these fish are required to  compete for their food in artificial farm ponds.

When you do finally look for these fish you're going to want to be careful because the older they are, the larger and stronger they are. Even if you can reel it in you're going to have a fight to get it done first.

## CHANNEL CATFISH REPRODUCTION

Reproduction for this fish begins in the summer when the water starts to get warmer. It needs to be around 75 degrees Fahrenheit for these fish to spawn. Once the female spawns however, she is no longer involved in the process. The male fish will rear the babies once they are born. In fact, the male has much to do with the process.

A male channel catfish will locate the nesting site somewhere dark and safe. It may also be a river wall, beaver dam or any other type of holes. These are safer spaces for the tiny eggs. Once the nesting site is found and made appropriately by the male the female will lay the eggs and move on. The male protects those babies from predators and becomes incredibly aggressive. This is actually the easiest time to catch one of these fish though it may be harder to reel in.

The male will even remove any unwanted matter from the nest during this time. The male is not engaged in regular feeding at this time (though they will attack your bait). They will not leave until the baby fish finally emerge.

# CHAPTER 2- THE BLUE CATFISH – THE SECOND BIG GIANT

Known in scientific circles as *Ictalurus Furcatus* the Blue catfish is another of the popular catfish found within the United States. Known also as the blue channel catfish, humpback catfish, great blue catfish, North American catfish or silver catfish, this one is the second most popular in the area.

## IDENTIFICATION

The blue catfish is slightly different from the first one we discussed. This fish is dark blue for one thing though unlike the channel catfish it is generally blue at all stages of life. It may have a slightly brownish skin combined with the blue however you will see the blue at all times as well.

In polluted water is the only time that you will see different colours in which case it will be almost albino-white.

Though this fish is very similar to the channel catfish it is not exactly the same. The differences discussed above apply of course. And this fish does not develop the speckles that a channel catfish will. Another difference is that these fish are heavier than the regular channel catfish we discussed previously. These could actually develop more than twenty pounds more and develop large bellies as a result. The largest blue catfish are typically found in well-oxygenated freshwater.

Younger fish of this type are typically more muscular and are also sleeker. They are found in small creeks or rivers. All of these blue catfish can be found in thirty different states of the country throughout both the north and south regions. The only requirement is a major river system and freshwater systems. These fish appear in clear and brackish water though there are some better regions for these fish including:

> James River
> Pamunkey River
> Staunton River
> Appomattox River
> Mattaponi River
> Rappahannock River
> Painatank River
> Potomac River
> Buggs Island Lake

## WHAT IT EATS

Similar to their brothers the channel catfish, the blue catfish will eat nearly anything in its path. The young even eat dead organic matter and plankton that can easily be found throughout freshwater. As they get older they tend to snack on living creatures such as insects or even small mammals such as mice.

## WHERE IT LIVES

Similar in reproduction to the channel catfish, this fish will breed in both clean and brackish water as it lives in both. Unlike the channel catfish the babies born from this fish tend to travel in schools rather than going off on their own after the nesting. The baby will likely grow about two inches in that first year of life.

# CHAPTER 3- THE FLATHEAD CATFISH – THE THIRD BIG GIANT

Finally we come to *Pylodictis Olivaris*, the flathead catfish and the third most common in the United States. In some states this is even considered to be an invasive species that has caused problems and danger for some of the native species in the area. These have been known to significantly deplete the number of native catfish and others within a body of freshwater.

## IDENTIFICATION

Just as you would expect from a fish known as a 'flathead' this fish does in fact have a rather wide and flat head. It has a lower jaw that is larger than the upper and can extend even more so. It also has a very square fin shape and is coloured in silver with green spots. These spots are

found throughout the entire body of the fish from the head to the tail.

Adult fish develop this spotting in an olive green while younger fish have jet black backs. They do not have the speckling that channel catfish do however.

## FEEDING AND REPRODUCTION

These fish will live, feed and reproduce the same as the blue and channel catfish that have been discussed above.

# PART 2: CASTING YOUR LINE

## BREAKING THE MYTHS ABOUT CATFISH

So when's the last time that you went catfishing? If you've never done so then you probably have a lot of misconceptions about it that you really need cleared up. That's because many people have a lot of ideas that they think are true about these fish and that they even pass on to newbies that are simply dead wrong. Here we'll discuss some of the more common ones and the truth of what you need to know.

**Myth #1: Dams are magnets for the biggest catfish.** Some say that these catfish are so huge that even professional divers fear being eaten if they dive near a dam.

**Fact:** As you can probably guess this is entirely false. Catfish do not grow so huge that they will eat a human. These are legends if you've ever heard of them and they have never once been proven by fact. A catfish within the United States will typically only grow to about twenty pounds and may not even be that large. The largest catfish you will see anywhere will be around 100 pounds and they definitely won't be eating a full-grown human either. Even though they may seem large enough they simply aren't capable of it.

**Myth #2: Catfish are only caught at night.**

**Fact:** Catfish feed any time of day though they feed the most during the night. Freshwater with no pollution or only a little pollution during the night are the very best for catching these fish however if you fish these same areas during the day they will still bite.

**Myth #3: Barbells of a catfish are poisonous.** These barbells or whiskers are said to cause intense agony for anyone who unwittingly touches them.

**Fact:** The barbells of a catfish do not contain any type of poison. In fact, they are completely harmless and you don't have to worry about touching them. These are used for tasting the water remember and for sensing vibrations. They can't hurt anyone.

The part of this fish to watch out for are the fins. These are incredibly sharp and will definitely cause pain. These fins could also be poisonous. If you don't know how to handle a catfish properly make sure you wear gloves. It will take practice before you can pick up a catfish with your bare hands without being cut by these sharp and potentially poisonous fins.

Just in case you do get a cut make sure that you wash it out quickly with warm, running water and use disinfectant as well. If the cut is deep go to a hospital immediately. No matter if the cut is shallow or deep keep an eye on it. Even if the fins aren't poisonous they could carry some form of bacteria that could cause you harm.

**Myth #4: Catfish swim in the worst water possible.** This is their favourite place to swim.

**Fact:** Catfish *can* swim in dirty and foul water however this is not where they prefer to be. It takes a lot of effort for these fish to survive in this type of water and it requires them to use all of their special abilities of sight, taste, smell and hearing. They do not, however, thrive in these conditions.

A catfish found in the worst water will typically be smaller than other fish and may even be unsafe to eat because of this. These fish can absorb chemical agents from the pollution within the water. In these cases they cannot be eaten by anyone.

**Myth #5: Odoriferous bait catches larger fish easier.**

**Fact:** Making your own bait is definitely not a bad thing and it definitely won't hurt your chances of catching a fish however smelly bait is not the same for the catfish as it is for us. For example you smell the bait and think it's awful however the catfish generally doesn't. Any type of bait that you would use for fishing for any other type of fish will still be effective with this one as well.

**Myth #6: Catfish are only caught in the summer.**

**Fact:** Catfish can be caught during the spring, summer and the fall. In the winter these fish are quite sluggish though they can still be caught. The most common times however are spring and summer. Depending on the activity of your area there may be plenty of movement within the catfish population throughout even the coldest months of the year. Good anglers have been known to catch them even during these times.

**Myth #7: Catfish will ignore shiny objects or metal.** Hooks must be invisible in order for the catfish to pay attention to them.

**Fact:** Catfish don't understand hooks. They don't know what they are or what they do. In fact, all they care about is the bait that you use. They also have no idea about 'shiny objects.' What you want to do is make sure that your hook is tied on properly and your bait is sufficiently tight so that the fish can't grab it and swim off because they will definitely try.

If you do catch a fish you want to record everything you can about it. Catfish have feeding patterns and prefer certain types of bait. They also tend to eat at similar times and in similar conditions frequently which vary by type of catfish. If you record all of this then you may be able to come back the same time and the same way another time and catch another catfish.

# CHAPTER 4- WHERE TO FIND THE CATFISH

So where will you find a catfish? Well you're not going to have a lot of difficulty figuring out the answer to that question. These fish are found in nearly any freshwater, polluted and even brackish water that you can find nearly everywhere in the world and certainly everywhere within the United States. Though specific types may be native only to specific areas there is likely at least one to be found in an area near you.

If you happen to catch a catfish that is in bad water conditions you should also know that these are likely not going to be very large. They also may not be safe for eating. They may not reach their highest numbers in these areas either which means it may even be harder to catch one.

Fishing within the United States? Look for clean, large bodies of freshwater. In these spaces you are most likely to find at least one of the big three and possibly even more. No matter where you are in the country your chances are extremely good though it's difficult to say if you'll be able to pull one in.

In semi-salt water you may find white catfish though most other breeds tend to avoid this type of water. The best place to fish is any type of freshwater. Whether it's clear or polluted these fish will live and spawn within these areas and you'll be able to find something.

# FINDING CATFISH IN THE US

Within the table that follows we'll tell you some of the best places that you can find some of the top types of catfish within the United States. They're found throughout the country so chances are you'll find an area that's near you on at least one of the lists you'll find here. Species that are less popular such as the bullhead and white catfish are included here as well.

| Catfish Species | Local Range |
|---|---|
| **Channel catfish** | <ul><li>*Rocky Mountains*</li><li>*Appalachian Mountains*</li><li>*Hudson Bay*</li><li>*Gulf of Mexico*</li><li>*Most states in the US (through assisted introduction in freshwater systems)*</li></ul> |
| **Blue catfish** | *At least 29 states are home to the blue* |

|  | *catfish, including:* |
|---|---|
|  | <ul><li>*South Dakota*</li><li>*Texas*</li><li>*Washington*</li><li>*Florida*</li><li>*Mexico*</li><li>*Guatemala*</li><li>*Belize*</li><li>*Mississippi*</li><li>*Ohio*</li><li>*Missouri*</li><li>*Oregon*</li><li>*California*</li><li>*Arizona*</li><li>*Colorado*</li><li>*Maryland*</li><li>*Virginia*</li><li>*South Carolina*</li></ul> |
| **Flathead catfish** | <ul><li>*Central American regions*</li><li>*Mississippi*</li><li>*Mobile*</li><li>*Rio Grande*</li><li>*Great Lakes*</li><li>*Mexico (some regions)*</li><li>*Arizona*</li></ul> |

| | |
|---|---|
| | <ul><li>*California*</li><li>*Colorado*</li><li>*Florida*</li><li>*Georgia*</li><li>*Idaho*</li><li>*Oregon*</li><li>*Pennsylvania*</li><li>*North Carolina*</li><li>*South Carolina*</li><li>*Virginia*</li><li>*Washington*</li><li>*Wyoming*</li></ul> |
| ***Ameirus catus* or the true white catfish** (should not be confused with flatheads or blue catfishes) | <ul><li>*New York*</li><li>*Gulf of Mexico*</li><li>*Alabama*</li><li>*Mississippi*</li><li>*California*</li><li>*Connecticut*</li><li>*Illinois*</li><li>*Indiana*</li><li>*Kentucky*</li><li>*Maine*</li><li>*Massachusetts*</li><li>*Nevada*</li><li>*New Hampshire*</li></ul> |

|  | <ul><li>Ohio</li><li>Oregon</li><li>Pennsylvania</li><li>Rhode Island</li><li>Washington</li><li>Puerto Rico</li><li>Great Britain</li></ul> |
|---|---|
| **Bullhead catfish** | <ul><li>Great Lakes</li><li>East Appalachian</li><li>Gulf of Mexico</li><li>Southern Canada</li><li>Northern United States</li><li>Central United States</li><li>Southern United States</li></ul> |

## The Best Spot to Catch That Catfish

So how do you get that giant catfish to take a bite on your line? Well you need to find the perfect place to fish. We've spent some time talking about how these fish are found in nearly any water and you can find them everywhere but that doesn't mean that some spots aren't a little better than others. In this section we'll talk about some of those best spots for catching a catfish.

We're going to focus on two specific bodies of water; lakes and rivers. These are where most of the catfish will be and these next two sections will tell you exactly where within these ranges you and your boat or you and your line should be waiting for that giant fish.

## PERFECT SPOTS IN THE RIVER

**Tailraces by Dams:** Before and during summer these are some of the best places to look for catfish. You want to look below the tailrace for one thing but the strong flow of water will draw in these fish during these times until you almost can't lose. This happens for two reasons; first there is a feeding frenzy where the catfish are seeking out more food and second because dams often obstruct spawning sights and the catfish will be trapped their on their way to spawn.

**Rock Dikes:** A rock or wing dike is created when structures are put in to control the widening of rivers and streams. These narrow the water and direct it towards the centre instead of outward. As a result, the current is slowed down and smaller fish tend to gather in these narrow channels. The catfish tend to travel to these areas because the food is readily available and easy to catch.

Small pools are the best when located by these rock dikes because they are spaces where the smaller fish and animals tend to congregate. Therefore they are also the places were large, strong catfish like to congregate. The smaller catfish are unable to compete with the larger ones which means that you're more likely to get a big fish in these areas.

**Tributary Mouth:** Do you know where the mating rituals of fish begin? Right at the mouth of the tributary. That means that at any time of year you will be able to find these catfish spawning or getting ready to spawn. The deep pools and clear water attract fish of all types which means you'll have fun even if you choose to catch something else for the day. This is nearly as easy as catching fish in a barrel. With so many there you'll only have to worry about fighting them into your boat or up on shore.

**Bends:** A bend within the river is an area where the water is traveling in two directions at once. In most areas the water travels the 'path of least resistance' however when it reaches a bend this isn't the case. Part of the water goes toward the least resistance however the outside bend of the water travels in the opposite direction. A tiny pool is created that flows in its own direction.

If you find a bend you can sit right by it. This is a great place to fish because the counter current tends to cause holes within the river bank. These holes are perfect for nesting catfish. The outside bend is also perfect for the smaller insects and mammals that catfish like to eat. That means you will be right next to a place where catfish could be swarming.

Trees are even better, at least fallen trees are. This is because the food presence increases even more in these conditions. Catfish will definitely be found in an outside bend with fallen trees. You could hardly ask for a better place to stop and wait.

**Bridges:** A bridge is a manmade structure and it's built to resist the water current pulling and pushing at its beams. As a result, small pools form around the base of those concrete pilings and allow smaller bait fish to breed or rest. Larger catfish then come to these areas for feeding.

This area is best if you have sonar equipment that will detect the groups of fish. When you find a large grouping you'll want to cast out your line parallel to the river and with the current. This is how you'll get the best chances for catching that elusive, giant catfish.

**Drifting Log Piles:** Look for exactly what you think, driftwood floating on the top of the water or next to the bank. These are areas where smaller fish and small mammals like to group and that means they are areas where bigger catfish like to do their hunting. They also form a great shelter for fish of all types to escape from the sun.

The problem with these log piles is that they are physical barriers to your fishing expedition. You need to be careful of how you cast your line so that when you hook a fish you can bring it in. The best thing to do is cast your line to the outside edge of the pile and let the current take it under. This way you can easily bring it back.

**Land Bars:** When the river erodes a section of the land into a narrow strip it's called a land bar. The area is actually made up of two land bars with a strip of water in between them. The strip is slow-moving and attracts small fish and animals because of that. It also provides shallow water for leeches and molluscs. As a result, these are areas where catfish will frequent as well. You'll be able to find them hunting for themselves here.

Within the Mississippi River and the Arkansas River there are plenty of these that attract shellfish who enjoy laying their eggs within these narrow strips. When they hatch in the spring catfish come from far and wide to feast on the easy prey.

**Boulders:** You may not think this is the best place to fish for anything but these are actually an excellent place to fish for any type of predatory fish. That's because the smaller fish use boulders and other areas as a hiding place from those big fish. Therefore the big fish go there to try and get the little fish out. Not only that but catfish tend to spawn in areas with shelter and hiding spaces like boulders so you could potentially find them nesting as well.

One problem you may have with fishing near boulders is that they are not always easy to spot from above the water. You'll want to watch out for boulder crowns or use tracking equipment to locate these under the water. They are prime spaces for schools of little fish during the summer which means that catfish tend to love them as well. There's nothing easier than catching dinner that's also eating its dinner. After all boulders are great for the plankton that smaller fish feed on.

Put your line in a low light area or wait until it gets darker. Also look for areas where the current is pushing against the boulder because these are where most of the hungry catfish will be. A good sinker is imperative as these allow your line to get into the deeper water. Being too close to the sun is not attractive to them and they tend to sink deeper during the daylight hours.

**River Chutes:** A chute is a narrow path or tunnel and a river chute is much the same. If there is an obstruction in or near the centre of the water it can cause a split within the current. These change the water current and attract some of the biggest catfish around. These fish are in the deep water near the upstream portion of the chute and they tend to be at the bottom of the water.

You want to make sure your line sinks all the way. You'll catch some of the biggest fish around this way.

## AMAZING SPOTS IN THE LAKE

**Wind-Battered Lake Shores:** If you see the flags standing straight out and the trees bending with the hard wind then you want to get started checking the lakes for catfish. With the harsh wind comes movement of plankton and smaller fish. These fish are seeking out their bait which is pushed toward the banks. The catfish then follow along to that bank as well making them easier for you to catch.

**Bottom Channels:** Every body of water connects in some way and some fashion to the sea. This is done through a network or channels. These channels are small and attract smaller fish which, in turn, attract catfish. Those catfish are easiest found right in the junction of a couple channels though you'll need a sonar tracker to help you find them.

**Banks of Overflowing Lakes:** When the water gets too high or there's too much rainfall then the lakes get full all the way to the top. When this happens the current and volume of water push the fish along faster. Shallow areas near the banks of these lakes turn into mini-pools and ponds themselves and smaller fish and catfish alike are attracted to these areas for food.

**Riprap:** This act somewhat like a bridge in that it's a manmade structure however these are used to keep the water from eroding the banks. These also provide shade and slower moving water for some of the smaller fish. In turn, large catfish tend to come along to feast on the leeches and shellfish that appear throughout the area. You'll want to look for small pools of water as your best spot to fish.

## TECHNIQUES FOR GETTING THAT FISH

So now we've gone through what catfish are and how they're different. We've also gone over where you can find them within rivers and lakes and exactly how to tell one species of catfish from another. What you need to know now is how to catch them. After all, what good is knowing all these things about catfish if you don't actually get to use that knowledge? Here in this section we'll talk about the four best ways to go about your fishing.

# CHAPTER 5- SIMPLE & STRATEGIC STILL FISHING

Do you know how still-fishing works? Chances are that you do. In fact this is one of the most common ways to fish for any type of fish. All you do is bait your hook, cast it out and wait. You just sit there and wait for the fish to come along and take that bait. It might rest just above the bottom or even at the bottom of the river, lake or other freshwater body of water. All you need to do is sit still and be patient.

With this method of fishing you may have to wait a long time. Your bait isn't moving which makes it easier for the catfish to find and catch but it does still have to figure out where it is and get there. It can sense that bait from a very long ways off and you don't know from where it has to travel to get to you. If you move around too much (or rather if your bait does) the catfish loses the scent and has to start over.

The point of still-fishing is to remain completely still. That means you don't twitch the line or pull it in and throw it back out. Your catfish can't lock onto the bait that way and it will give up. You can fish this way whether you're on the bank or on a boat but you'll need to make sure your boat is off so the motor doesn't mess with the vibrations in the water and scare the fish away.

If you're on the bank you'll want to find a really good area that you're sure will bring in some fish. You can't be traveling too much if you have all your gear and you're on foot. You also need to be sure that you're not moving too much and confusing that fish. A boat makes this easier because you can find the perfect spot even if it's in the middle of the water.

1. Keep your boat and your line completely, 100% still while you're fishing this way. Two anchors tend to work better than one as they keep your boat even more still and give you an even better chance. Even one anchor can help but one at each end of the boat keeps it from swaying back and forth.

2. If you can use a boat then you definitely should. These allow you to keep searching the water to find the perfect spot. You'll be able to locate the prime spots to at least give it a shot. You want to

give any spot you find a chance to produce some great catfish. You want to be close to the group so they can sense your bait but not too close or you could scare them off simply by casting that line.

3. Finding the best places near the riverbank are also important. If you don't have a boat you need to be able to locate these more easily. Again these are the areas with higher density of catfish which might be areas with rocks but it might not. You should scout out the areas as much as you can before fishing there.

4. All those strange spots in the water where there are boulders, stumps, fallen trees, etc. are the perfect place to search for catfish. These are the areas where they love to gather because the food is easy. You might have a slightly more difficult time of it with your line so close to these obstacles but your chances of catching a catfish are much higher.

5. Dams are the best for in the springtime because this is when migration and catfish runs are in full swing. You'll be able to find catfish upstream because this is where they spawn. Remember what we said about tailwater.

6. Having the right rod is important also. You want to have at least 10 and preferably 14 inches long. Make sure it's the right weight so you can move it easily and also that it's strong enough to put up a fight with a catfish that could weigh more than twenty pounds. Sinkers should weigh at least 8 ounces. This is because you want your bait to sink down to the catfish instead of floating close to the surface. Bell sinkers, egg sinkers and 3-way rigs are your best options.

7. Still waters are the best place to look for catfish. This is where their food tends to sit and that means it's the best place (and the easiest) to find them. This is true in strong current or slow water as well as areas that have both. You need to make sure you move your line slowly if you do at all. That means only three or four feet away (on the current) every quarter of an hour. This allows you to get the best space without having to move too much physically. Your line will be doing most of the work.

8. Fishing piers have been built in many different areas. These are areas where you can fish that are built right in the water. They also allow you a better chance to catch a fish. These platforms allow large numbers of people to fish in the same area and they also allow for families and children

because they are large enough to accommodate large groups. These are also structures which imitate the physical landmarks that attract catfish. They may have fallen trees or boulders underwater which are clearly marked above for you to aim your line.

# CHAPTER 6- DRIFT FISHING FROM THE BOAT

This is one of the more active forms of fishing that you could try. It's going to require you to do a little more moving and definitely won't bore you like some people experience with still-fishing. You'll be moving along a little more and you'll definitely want to have a great bobber for this method of fishing.

When it's a little colder outside it tends to be best to use this method. That's because the fish tend to disperse more than ever. They tend to travel in groups in the warmer weather but when it gets cold they start to get a bit more sluggish. If the freshwater that you're fishing in is a little over or under full then you'll want to try out this method as well because the changes in water level move the fish around.

If you have a boat you'll have the best chance with this method though it can be done on the riverbank. The great thing with drift-fishing is that you can use one or more different rods at the same time. Some fishing boards will restrict the number of rods you can use at a time so check with your local board before you start. You may be able to use two or more rods during this time.

In drift-fishing you want your line and the bait to slowly drift toward the catfish. You'll move the bait through the water toward the fish as they are scattered throughout the water. You'll have the best chance to attract the fish to you. If you have a motor you can use it slowly to drift in the direction that you want. If you don't have a motor you'll only be able to drift the way that the current is moving.

One way to ensure that your rods stay where they need to be is to use a fixed clamp. These keep your line from being torn away and also keep you from having to hold on to all of your rods. This helps you secure the lines and rods to the boat. Another method is to mount the rods to the boat where they will be permanently attached. You want to make sure in this case you are attaching them in the arcs at the end of the boat.

Another great thing about using multiple lines is that you can use several different baits and also several different depths. You'll want to use a different type of bait with each of your rods, ideally up to four rods. You're also going to want four different depths of the water including the bottom, middle and barely below the surface. You can choose a fourth depth as well.

When you get a bite (after you pull in the fish) you'll want to take note of which line, depth and bait was the one to get the bite. This will enable you to find the best place to keep fishing later. Try to reorient your lines after that first bite so you get them in the right area and at the right depth. You'll know where to go next time this way as well because you'll have the information you'll need.

Another thing you're going to want for drift-fishing is a float-rig. This can be done with a pencil weight or trolling-sinker. The pencil weight works best for seeking the bottom of the body of water while trolling-sinkers work best for middle or high depths. This enables you to get the best range and helps you get a bite and catch your catfish.

When you use your boat you're going to want to experiment a little with your motion. Of course the purpose of drift-fishing is to be moving so you want your boat to keep moving. The right speed is going to be a little bit different based on where you are specifically. A general rule of thumb is that the clearer the water you're fishing in the faster your boat is able to move because the catfish will be able to find your bait faster and easier in clear water.

Of course you'll want to track everything once again. So when you catch that catfish and reel it in make note of which way you were going on the water and how fast you were sending your boat along. This will help you catch more. You want to make sure you don't slow down or speed up as you go and also that you don't change direction because this will throw off the fish that are trying to catch your bait and sabotage your efforts. When there are no more catfish biting in the direction you're traveling then you'll want to readjust.

If you're on the riverbank use a bobber and try to locate the best area where catfish like to gather. Let your line float and keep letting the line out so that it's carried downstream by the current. Even on the bank of the river you're going to want to try out different depths of water. Keep the line taut and don't let it get too slack. That's what makes your line difficult to control and it also makes it so easy for the catfish to get away from you.

# CHAPTER 7- EASY LIMBLINING FROM THE RIVERBANK

This type of fishing is simple and great for use during the night. You're going to use a technique of hooking your line to a tree limb. For this task you need a strong line and a very strong tree limb as well. This is what keeps the fish from getting away after you catch it. All you're going to need to do is go and pick up the line with the fish.

These lines need to be stronger than a regular line. You're going to need a braided line of at least 25 pounds. You'll also want an extra weight on the hook for powerful currents in freshwater bodies of water. This will keep your line where you want it to be rather than moving it around with the current.

This method, like drift-fishing, allows you to use more than one line at a time. You can set up these lines as much as you want you'll only want to make sure that you know where each one is so it can easily be found again. If you don't catch anything or even if you do you need to be able to find the lines quickly to pull them in or pull them down.

The best limbs are thick and green because they have strength and they won't break. Those catfish are strong remember and a brittle limb will simply break under the stress of a fight with that catfish. The thick strong limbs can take the pressure while you get to the line and pull it in.

There are also some special assemblies that allow you to attach your line and keep it moving properly. Using a limb attached within the riverbank will allow you to do the same as you did with the trees. This works best when you don't have the right type of tree limbs to attach your line too.

# CHAPTER 8- GET OUT AND START NOODLING

So now we come to the most difficult but one of the oldest known methods of fishing. This one uses your bare hands to snatch the catfish out of the water. This can be extremely difficult because you have to be able to literally reach into the water and pull out a catfish without bait and without a hook or any type of line. It takes a lot of practice and a whole lot of work.

Anyone who attempts this is definitely proving their abilities. Any angler will have a very good respect for those who do this because it can be dangerous as well as difficult. This is because snakes and other dangerous animals could be hiding in the same place as a catfish and that means you could end up bitten or injured.

Grabbing a catfish isn't terribly dangerous as you don't need to worry about being bitten. You will have to struggle with the fish itself which is very strong and definitely not going down without a fight. These fish are slippery and strong which means they will continue moving as much as possible to get away.

The best place to start with noodling is near the bank of the river. You'll want to reach into the holes located there and find the head of the catfish. Never grab the body or the fins of the fish as you could be injured this way. Instead you want to grab the jaws or gills. Remember these fish have no teeth and therefore can't bite you. Then you'll want to pull it right up to the surface.

Canes can be an excellent idea for this type of fishing because they ensure that what's in the hole is actually a catfish before you reach in and get bit by something more dangerous. You'll be able to choose the level of water that you want and can go into deeper or shallower waters. You can even dive for fish at the bottom of the river. If you're noodling you want to make sure you have a friend with you that can help you in your task. This can be very difficult and potentially dangerous after all.

# CHAPTER 9- BAITING THE HOOK

Nearly everything that you can think of is possible as bait for these catfish. That's because catfish will eat nearly everything including soap. The Big Three will eat anything live or cut though it's recommended that you use live bait if you're using limblining.

The best way to find out the perfect bait is to talk with someone in the area and find out from them. Biologists tend to know catfish in the area and can tell you what the best idea is. There are commercial baits available for each specific fish you could think of as well so you can check out what is offered within your area specifically for a catfish. Or you can find your own bait in just about any type of smaller fish or plankton.

## THE PERFECT HOOKS AND SINKERS

There are several different hooks and sinkers available for use and each one has its own uses and benefits. Here is a table that will help you out with determining the perfect sinker and hook for your needs.

| Hook Type | Description |
| --- | --- |
| Barbless hook | If you're looking to put the fish back this is the best option to use. |
| Spring-wound hook | If you need to use a soft bait that won't stay on a normal hook this one can be used instead. |
| Circle hooks | Probably the most popular version of catfishing hooks available, this one is able to grab onto the jaw of the fish. |
| Shad gut hook | This is a very universal hook that holds different types of bait and grabs onto the jaw of the fish like a circle hook. |
| Double-needle hook | If you have a soft bait this hook attaches more easily. |
| Baitholder hook | These look like round hooks but they're actually capable |

| | |
|---|---|
| | of holding soft or hard bait even in strong currents. This is because of the thorns on the length of them. |
| Weedless hook | If you're going to be fishing in a messy area with trees then this hook keeps you from snagging them. |

| Sinker Type | Description |
|---|---|
| Barrel sinker | These are likely what you think of when you first think of a bobber. They're quite common and move along the entire line. They don't work well in strong currents however. |
| Bell sinker | Perfect for drift-fishing these sinkers keep your bait from bouncing at all. |
| Walking sinker | These are some of the easiest sinkers to cast and they work great for drift-fishing as well. |
| Bullet sinker | These are shaped similar to a bullet and keep your line from getting snagged if you go drift-fishing. |

# CHAPTER 10- THINGS TO REMEMBER

1. Catfishing in the winter requires a little more work because the fish are scattered more rather than traveling in groups. You're going to want to use fresh fish and aim for deep water if you plan to fish during these times.

2. In the summer you want to make sure you know the temperature of the water you're fishing in. If it's between 75 and 80 degrees Fahrenheit then the fish are spawning and you're more likely to get the really big fish.

3. Your rod should be at least 10 feet long for fishing off the bank.

4. Believe it or not catfish will actually eat chicken liver and not only will they eat it but they actually love it. They have a lot of juice but remain firm as well. With this for bait you can get your catfish from even further away.

5. Soap that is unscented can actually be cut up into small squares and used as bait. It has to be unscented but fish love to eat this stuff and it's something cheap you have around the house.

6. Late afternoon is the best time if you're going fishing because the bigger fish tend to move more in the darkness. Limblines are even better in the high traffic areas.

7. In water that's going to move quickly you want to make sure you have a rod with a flexible tip. The problem with straight rods is that the fish grabs on and the rod moves sharply to keep with the current. If the rod bends the fish is more likely to hold on because they don't get the immediate snap.

8. Remember when you were a kid fishing with hot dogs? Well those are actually quite effective for catfish bait. It's not going to bring them in because there isn't enough of a smell but it will attract them if dropped down in their group.

9. Look in large bodies of water for the biggest fish. The smaller ponds are good for smaller fish but the biggest ones are hidden in the lakes. These are the ones that will win you trophies.

10. If you fish in areas with riprap you'll want crayfish or minnows for bait and probably circle hooks as well. These best suit the area and the types of fish you'll find there.

11. If you plan on using worms like the average beginning fisher you'll want to make sure they're covered when you set them down. If you stick them in a can and forget about them they tend to get away on you. Use a piece of fabric or soil to prevent this.

# ABOUT THE AUTHOR

Hello, my name is Bowe Chaim Packer and I like to see myself as an open, *"wear my heart out on my sleeve"* kind of guy.

Some of the most important things to me in my life are:

- Laughing
- Kissing
- Holding hands
- Being playful
- Smiling
- Talking deeply with others
- Being loved
- Loving others
- Changing the world one person at a time (if my presence in your life doesn't make a difference then why am I here?) Hmmmmm, maybe that is a topic for another book. ;-)
- Learning from others (although often times I first resist). However, don't give up on me….
- Sharing ideas (no matter what they might be)
- Learning about others via most forms of contact.

- Traveling – hello, of course – almost forgot one of my favorite pass times.

Remember, LIFE is a journey for each and every one of us. We must never forget the things that are important to us or lose sight of what makes us happy.

CPSIA information can be obtained
at www.ICGtesting.com
Printed in the USA
LVHW062249290523
748288LV00037BA/1297